ART OF ESCAPE

Mina Gorji was born in Tehran and grew up in London. She
lives in Cambridge where she is a lecturer in the English
Faculty, Cambridge and a fellow of Pembroke College. Her
published work includes a study of John Clare and essays
on awkwardness, mess, weeds and rudeness. Her poems
have appeared, among other places, in *Magma*, *PN Review*,
London Magazine, *The International Literary Quarterly* and
New Poetries V.

ART OF ESCAPE

MINA GORJI

CARCANET

First published in Great Britain in 2020 by
Carcanet
Alliance House, 30 Cross Street
Manchester M2 7AQ
www.carcanet.co.uk

A CIP catalogue record for this book is
available from the British Library.
ISBN 978 1 78410 882 3

Book design by Andrew Latimer
Printed in Great Britain by SRP Ltd, Exeter, Devon

The publisher acknowledges financial
assistance from Arts Council England.

CONTENTS

For my parents, Naheed and Taghi,
and for Ladan and Sousan,
Zach, Zarina and Ariana,
with love

THE WASP

who makes no honey gave us ink.
In early spring oak galls appear:
darkening in autumn
they gestate.

Emerging into English light,
this tiny emigrant
was smuggled in Aleppo oak –
an alien acorn.

CHARANGO

The Armadillo lives alone
in armour,
plates of dermal bone,
scale lapping scale
in compact rows –
protective carapace
prized for resonance.

Blowball, Puff-Ball, *pis-en-lit*,
Priest's Halo –
Sin in the Grass,
one tiny spore
proliferates –
an empire spread on air; dandelion –
blown across oceans by ill winds,
weed and bitter remedy –
chicoria, pissabet,
bittera tzelaut.

MIGRANTS

They shot them in the fields –

'Skylarks that sung to Nazis
are not welcome here'.

Territories of the heart contract
as music's mapped;
song-flight's fleshbound and distressed –
a small brown bird
in alien corn.

BITTERN

it thrives
in brackish water
where the sea has broken in –
in marshes and on river banks –
edges of solid ground.
When danger comes
it imitates the reeds,
sticking its head up straight
and swaying in the wind.
A nervous bird, more often heard than seen,
its hollow boom
was heard at night
in ancient and in empty times –
in Nineveh and Babylon.

EXIT

Airport security was tight
the day we left,
my sister in a pram and I
holding my mother's hand.
She was heavy
with gold coins and cash,
rings, necklaces,
anything of worth
that could be snuck, hid,
stuffed in a sock or slipped
into the secret of a heel.
The bigger things
we left behind.
Pinched hard,
my sister screamed
so loud
the chadored guards
just scowled,
and waved us through,
unfrisked.

TEHRAN

my great aunt's house –
the upstairs spare room
now unlocked:
old boxes, packed
in haste, and left:
our mothballed futures
gather dust.
Outside in the boulevard
they're wiping lipstick
off girls' mouths
with tissues wrapped
round razor blades.

SACRIFICE

We'd seen them led into the yard,
tethered near the little pond
where my grandmother used to sit,
or rather, squat,
shelling broad beans into a sieve,
or spreading mint
on sheets of cloth to dry.
She'd hollow out a watermelon
and we'd drink the juice,
and sail the empty skins.
We knew why they'd been brought –
and so we set them free,
untied the ropes and watched them
start and shamble,
gawky, panicking.
Those white goats are upside
down, throats slit,
hanging from a tree.

ESCAPE?

He asked *'where you from, ma'am?'*
and when I said 'Iran',
he hugged me and replied
'You made it'
with such kindness
I didn't have the heart to ask
'But do you know
the lizards in Persepolis?
the mountain ranges
stretching into snow?
the taste of *kharboozeh?*
that final feeling when the lift doors close?

ABLATION

Spring might not reach
the hazels on the river bank:

their branches, lopped,
pile up against the snow.

Stark vertical
the devastated trunks
remain –

and yet they're hazels still,
despite it all.

THE SONG OF THE REED
after Rumi

Inside the reed
a wainscot moth
winters, as an egg.

Inside the reed
a secret,
longing for the wind.

Inside the reed
a message
gathers into ink.

PERSEPOLIS

They say the Lion and the Lizard keep
The Courts where Jamshýd gloried and drank deep.

Shaded by a parasol
the king looks out:
deserted plains,
the sky,
the hawks,
the yellow flowers,
a lizard darting over stones –
nothing else remains.

BEARINGS

the heart
of the compass
is always still –
despite the restless skitter
of the needle tip.

PITSEOLAK

I draw what I have never seen –
the monsters and the spirits,
the old ways,
and how we lived
before the white men came.

I travelled in a boat
with sails
made from the intestine of whale,
and fished for halibut
with silver hooks,
and hunted caribou.

I came to recognize
the gainful loss –
and could interpret
all its sounds –
the questioning
of birds at sea,
the crack of ice,
the coming thaw.

Living a life
between these shores –
I, born inside a sealskin tent,
hear on the radio
two men have landed on the moon.

PEARL DIVER

*'Young women today don't like the sea as much as we do, they lack courage
and don't want to get their skin darkened by working in the water.'*
— Kotoyo Motohashi, Pearl Diver, or 'Ama'

Upturned
fishing boats –
cormorants
dry their wings.

An empty tub
for abalone,
cuttlefish,
or octopus
settles on the woodblock waves.

One long breath
and Kotoyo descends,
like her mother
and her grandmother
before her.

Currents stir the kelp;
water murkens:
Kotoyo
can barely see her hands –

or the knife
that separates
sea-bed from oyster shell.
She is last of the Ama
of Shirahama.

THE WHALEBONE HOUSE

In June, a storm of hail and rain
brought winter to the London streets,
and people came
by water, horse and coach, on foot,
to see the whale.

At low tide it appeared at last,
and after many hours
encompassed round
with harping irons,
the whale was killed.

The quiet of the whalebone house
agreed with me –
and so I waited there
and watched –
and found a comfort in the forms –

vertebrae arranged in rows
around the door and window frames,
patterns out of porous bone with flint,
bright cut, and cobble stone.

ON THE STRANDLINE

slipper limpet,
razorshell,
hornwrack, samphire,
mermaid's glove,
and starfish – storm-script –
stranded all along the coast.
I find one that's still alive –
and throw it back.
This is not the time for tears.

MERMAID

caught alive
just off the Shetland Isles,
two feet in length
and finned along the spine;
her tiny hands
are webbed,
the lower portion
of her breast
scales into
a slippery tail.
Only her voice
escaped.

KAMASUTRA (THE SUBSIDIARY ARTS)

To make designs
on courtyard floors
with rice powder and sand
is seventh of the sixty-four
arts to hold desire.
Cutting patterns
out of leaves
is number five.
Forty-third
teaching mynah birds
and parrots how to talk.
And if you master repartee,
sign language, foreign tongues,
and practice all these arts of love –
there's no room left
for emptiness,
no time
for broken hearts.

SERENADE

The female fruit fly cannot sing
but she can recognise
the warm vibrato
of a mate:

a serenade
not issued from the tongue –
but from the high-pitched trill
of hidden wings;

if clipped
he grows invisible
to her. They can collide a thousand times
inside this glassy chamber,

but caught
in unnatural silence
she is insensible,
bears no fruit.

REINCARNATION

Its coronet
distinctive
as a thumbprint,
the seahorse –
Hippocampus –
shares – or rather gave its name
to a tiny part of human brain
located on the floor
of the lateral
ventricle,
that governs short
term memory
and spatial navigation.
Slow-moving,
and a poor swimmer,
it relies
on camouflage
to escape
reincarnation
as paperweight
or tacky souvenir.
With luck, perhaps,
it might,
dissolved
into a tonic
against human
impotence,
be born again
with legs.

THE RAT MAN

inspected the evidence:
gnawed floorboards, holes,
what remained of a chilli plant
(nothing but a pale green stump).
He explained the pros and cons
of poison, glue, a snapping trap.
We pictured a determined rat,
single, hungry, brownish grey.
The Rat Man finished his tea.
He was dreaming
of the rat goddess
in her temple in Rajasthan,
its ancient marble pillars
and solid silver doors.

APPETITE

For weeks it sulked,
rejected all my offerings –
the mice, the meat, the long-tailed rat,
even the rabbit
failed to stir its appetite.
One night I woke to find it stretched
along the length of me,
rigid and quite still.
It looked across the bed unblinkingly.
I knew at once –
the snake would have to go:
from head to head
and tip of tail to toe,
my ambitious pet
was sizing its next meal.

CRUSTACEA

They don't have a heart, you said.
We moved on to dessert –
further apart.
The conversation turned
to horseshoe crab.
Manoeuvre past
its unimpressive claws,
infiltrate
the armament
of shell –
you'll find
the blood runs copper blue –
unique.
It's Haemocyanin
Such a capacity for fact.

Along the coast
the horseshoe crab
scuttles away,
alone in the Creation.

OCTOPI

There are cephalopods
alive today –
enormous creatures
have been
photographed.
But none has ventured
to the coast,
excepting
as a carcass,
until now.
Classified with oysters,
zoologically,
they have an eye
that is mammalian –
almost human:
its colour changes
reveal intimate feelings:
red for anger,
black for envy
blue for fear;
its eyelids
give a sensitive
and varied look,
not like that
horror-struck
expression
of a fish
whose two
round eyes
are fixed.

POLIPO

On coasts
laid bare
by sea,
tentative,
without a shell,
you may see
an octopus
cautiously advance –
one tentacle
in front
of the other.
Exposed
in grandeur
and in mass
(but not
for long)
it seeks out
shelter,
nestling
in the tiniest crack,
conceals itself
with pebbles,
carapaces,
shells.

Secret histories
in stone –
sometimes a filigree
of leaf and bone,
sometimes the wind
will shape itself
in isotope,
lifetime in a flash
of thermoluminescence.

SPIRIT GROUNDS

Here in the spirit's burial ground
all is emptiness and rock.
I waited and I watched
for it to pass.

The ground was dry:
I prayed for rain,
for mercy in the channels of the heart.

And slowly, shoots –
and tiny pinks uncurled;
such gentleness
from what seemed heedless rock.

Here in the dark –
a sudden glint:
the rock remembers
ancient sea.

Glaciers of salt –
the dry black mountains range –
salt that glistens, white,
without the gift of thaw.

But nature is resilient –
even here
the *halophytes*
survive.

AMARYLIS

It needs to be forgotten
somewhere dark and cool,
remote from expectation,
given up for dead,
before it can
remember
to issue its
green tongue,
and scarlet
petal bells.

NOW AT LAST

the rains have passed:

in the trees
the birds resume;

the grass
shares its secret,

the snail
puts out its horns –

perhaps the heart
can trust again.

SOLITARY BEES

These little miners, masons, cutters
take such care
to dig, to hollow
and to line their nests
with pieces neatly cut
from willow herb,
rose petal or rose leaf;
then fill them up
with nectar and with pollen
for their young,
and then, with mud
or chewed-up leaf glue,
delicately seal them shut.

TINEOLA BISSELLIELLA

Nibbling sneakthief!
How I've been deceived –
how carefully
I placed these offerings –
lavender and cedarwood,
conkers, camphor,
naphthalene –
you preferred cashmere,
the comfort of grandmother's furs,
a hand-me-down kaftan
with intricate embroideries –
pink and blue and yellow flowers.

I should have known that morning
when the magpies tapped
the window pane,
tapped, then shat
a warning, bright on glass.

Or when, a few months later,
I found a dead wasp
on my pillow,
and the next night,
another dead wasp.

Or when, falling asleep,
I was stung by a third
(already dead).

They found the nest,
pale, intricate,
almost beautiful
in the roof
above my bed.

It had been growing slowly
over many years
and only now
revealed itself.

You used to say
I was born lucky –
born with a tooth.
How you would comfort me
with prayers, and blow them over me
like kisses, to keep me safe.

HIVE

The wooden floor is polished
the door is painted black
no footsteps clatter down the stair
this is the home of lack –

a house still cold and comfortless
as winter turns to spring
its windows blank, insensible
to any living thing.

Quiet drifts through empty rooms
as I stand listening –
and cosy in their attic nest
the wasps are whispering.

NIGHT GARDEN

Late at night the slippered feet
move stealthy over torchlit grass.
The night air gathers into dew,
the silver scissors hunt out slugs.

Light shines through the bean leaves –
They're perforated into lace;
pearlescent tracery appears,
and here and there
bright snips of jet.

Descending towards Triplow
the chalky land
is lost
in a brown
and gravelly loam,
lying upon gravel:
there, in warm
and gentle soil,
you might find love
or *cinquefoil*.

POPPIES

The solstice poppies
prophesied good things,
and Saturn's playful transiting
of Venus augured well.
A pair of magpies
chattered overhead,
and all around us
wheat was ripening:
the world, it seemed, aligned,
for us to join
its patterning.

we look up:
so many shooting stars!
A flash, and then they seem to slow:
one after another,
flash and fade.

These are not stars
but landing lights –
not blazing out,
but coming home.

MORNING STAR

No trace is left,
no record of that brightness –
light has faded into light,
dawn into day.
The time for hope is past;
the planet only disappears
from sight.

HOW TO WRITE WITH METEORITE

after Cornelia Parker

Heating up a meteorite
on the little kitchen stove:
center of a universe
of kettle, pan and oven glove.
She lands it glowing
on the map –
and presses
so it makes a mark,
and paper streets
turn ashy dark:
sky-sign diminishes
in singe.

POEM FOR THE EQUINOX

All summer long
the salt-fear sank
deep in the bone,
shock in the jaw
like a primal curse,
and the constant ache.
But now at last
it is the autumn equinox,
such grace:
dahlias in rows
and rows
and I
swinging in a hammock
in the afternoon sun,
at the end of summer;
the dahlias in rows,
and children,
playing in the grass.

The planet cools
against the edge of space:
to go beyond
our atmosphere
and move among the stars
appeals to you.
The thought
of all that emptiness,
of unknown, scentless galaxies,
makes me appreciate
the pull of earth,
these feet of clay.

ERIS

uninvited harbinger
of dissonance –
who cast her bitter apple to the world –
has just been discovered
orbiting our sun; –
a place at last
for havoc in the stars.

Every night the telescope reveals
another galaxy,
a faint star cluster near Sirius,
the Pleiades in Taurus,
spiraling Andromeda.
My heart turns to distant Eridanus,
winding river of stars,
path of souls:
every night
they are moving
further from us.

AT THREE YEARS OLD

your questions touch
the limits of imagining:
Where is the Other Country?
Do people there have legs?
– hold hands?
If this is heaven,
why can't they escape?

THE KÁRMÁN LINE

My spirit has been called
away from earth,
to this strange limbo
at the edge of atmosphere,
where meteors combust,
and black lights into blue,
Aurora Borealis forms –
and vacuum
turns to air.

THE TENACITY OF DUST –

lodging itself
between the window panes,
along the skirting boards,
on the forgotten,
underneath the bed –
even the lampshade furred.
The air is filled
with particles
of light.

POEM
for my grandfather

We'd wake up early
to watch surgery
on TV –
tiny incisions:
intimate,
but distant.
The heart
open,
the life
abstracted.

A VISION IN PECKHAM RYE

Standing there I saw,
or so it seemed,
the rivers of the world flow by,
and time moved in a different way
as they passed by.
And my worries disappeared
as I stood and watched
that slow majestic tide
of ladies in bright cloth
with heads held high.
And the fever and the fret,
the nagging thoughts of this and that,
all faded now as they went by.
No angels here,
a vision all the same,
of ladies wrapped in bright batik
and turbans of triumphant cloth,
some with babies,
some with heavy bags and sticks,
moving slow and graciously
along the road
in Peckham Rye.

ICE SHIP

At night the heavy ice ship docked,
packed tight with its cargo
of compacted fossil snow.
Towards morning it'll glisten
through windows of polished glass –
fishmonger panes rubbed bright
with vinegar and newspaper rags.
Sunlight silvers through,
picking sequin herring scales,
lifting like a pattern out of frost.

Crabs are the only living things
waiting on the silent ice.
Fish eyes are glassed over;
cod gills bloom black-red;
the cross-eyed long-fanged conger eel
is heavy now and still.
Secretly, the lobster
has given up the ghost:
suspended far from home, buried
in quartz ice – waiting to blossom
to molten pearl and vanish,
quicksilver to air.

Over the North Sea sunrise sits
heavy as oil slick, or a blessing.

THE ART OF ESCAPE

The great Houdini closed his eyes.
Imagining himself
inside the lock –
iron passageways
opened before him.
He felt his way along these dark canals
and out of a coffin
submerged in water,
or from a straightjacket, buckled
and suspended from a bridge,
like a giant man-moth.
Closing his eyes
he felt the night air
close against his skin:
even the outside
couldn't hold him long.

OXFORD RAGWORT

From Etna's cinder slopes
to the Botanic garden –
Senecio Squalidus
escaped;
it slipped out of its cultivated bed,
the ancient cemetery walls,
the city's bounds,
following the gaps
in paving stones,
the new-laid tracks
of railway lines,
south-east
along the clinker beds,
into the heart of London:
bomb craters,
burnt-out scrubland,
scorched earth again.

FORBIDDEN FRUIT

My first batch
of *Poplar-cap*, –
lightly fried,
on toast,
made me hesitate.
Dangers of the delicate:
the deadly *Web-cap*
(easily confused
with *Chantarelle*)
or *Avenging Angel*
whose pale green cap
can kill,
the glycosides
in *Bluebells*
and in *Buttercups*
that blister skin
and make the heart
erratic,
and *Hemlock*
that's so easy to mistake
for *Parsley, Fennel,*
Lady's Lace.

IN WHITE.

What is white? a swan is white
Sailing in the light.

Ghost white –
a tint of white
imagined colour
of a ghost.

My mother's hair
was never white.

Bone white –
hides stains
better than
white.

Blue-white
neutralised
with umber:
Echo.

White smoke:
a beautiful light
green with soft
tan undertones.

White smoke
Hex color: f5f5f5
hue: 0.00
saturation: 0.00
lightness value: 0.96.

First Light.

Shadow white.

ESCAPE,

/ɪˈskeɪp/
flee,
get free
like Daedalus
like Icarus.
Oute of youre lace
into the desert,
jump –
like electricity
escapes
when atmospheric pressure
is removed,
like leaves,
at the time of flowering,
escaping from their buds,
jump
or a spaceship
escaping from Earth
at 11·2 kilometres
a second
jump
elude,
escape
and lightly pass
the bitter pain
of purgatory,
the name of which
escapes me.

Two brothers left Tblisi, Gorjistan, and travelled to the desert in Iran. No-one knows why they left, or what they were escaping. They married two sisters and settled in Yazd. But their children moved out to the capital or followed trade routes to India.

My maternal grandparents in an army ship, leaving Madras for Liverpool, escaping the Djinn that took three of their children. They moved on to Edinburgh so grandfather could extend his training as a surgeon, FRCS. A few years later, 1947, Partition. They stayed in Britain.

Their own grandparents had left Iran for the wealth and seeming glamour of the British Empire – India, Hong-Kong, Singapore. They traded in opium and indigo, animal skins. Grandfather went to missionary school in Madras. They didn't use his real name, *Mohammad Taqui* – it sounded too foreign.

Grandmother was born in Singapore. Her teachers called her *Daisy*. Her name was *Shahtaj*. Tango was her favourite dance. Her grandfather, *M.A. Namazie*, had made a fortune in rubber. In 1930, he built one of the island's first cinemas, *The Capitol Theatre*. The *Straits Times* that year called it

> a thing of romance,
> a dream solidified.

It screened the first-run English language films. Once a week grandmother was driven there to watch a matinee. On the domed ceiling of the Capitol, sculptures of winged horses, a mosaic of the twelve zodiac signs. Romance. The Great Depression – the price of rubber fell. Namazie died of a heart attack. Grandmother's years at medical school were cut short by marriage. She left Singapore for India in 1936, five years before the Japanese invasion.

1971. My mother, recently married, travelling by plane from London to Tehran – she didn't feel as though she was escaping. Eight years later, flying back to London, she did.

Tehran, 1979. Outside my window, mountains. The highest, *Damavand.* Visiting my uncle north of the city, I fell into a drift of snow, chin deep. At school, in the playground, I stepped in the warm wet tar. Just to feel it underfoot, to mark its perfect glossy blackness. It clung to my shoe. Soon we would be leaving.

We could see it changing from the window of our apartment. Demonstrations. Tanks. Soldiers. We could hear chanting. There were blackouts. Sitting in our flat, surrounded by boxes and crates packed with antique furniture – dark wood carved with tiny Chinese figures, men with long beards, ladies under cherry trees, curling clouds, dragons. It had travelled from Singapore to India, India to London and then to Iran, part of my grandmother's and then my mother's *trousseau.* The delivery men wouldn't take it – no antiques could leave the country. They were tightening the borders. People grew ingenious – hid gold coins in jars of jam, jewellery in the hollow of a carved-out heel. Our toys were given to the local hospital – I knew that we were leaving.

London, SW13, 1980. At five years old, I dreamed of firing squads. Flinched when I saw policemen. But there was warmth and family and love. Masala omelette, sweet with fried onions. Rice pudding, golden with saffron.

45 Lowther Road. I felt safe in that house, with its greengage trees, the secret musty smell of garden shed, the bright pink and purple swirls, paisley patterns on the duvet that crackled static when we huddled underneath. She'd whisper prayers until we fell asleep and blow them over us, to keep us safe.

Patterns. The antique Persian carpet in my grandparents' house stretched into the afternoons. I used to jump between the different coloured panels, making up stories, dreaming. Tiny feet, treading over rooftops of a miniature world:

Cyprus trees and citadels,
>   palaces with copper domes,
>   leopard chasing antelope,
>   the moon in silver scimitar,
> gardens full of roses.
>   So many stories,
>   knotted into silk.

Persepolis. One of my relations met Agatha Christie walking in the ruins of Persepolis. When I visited, it was almost empty. Winged bulls. A lizard darting over sand. *They say the lion and the lizard keep / The courts where Jamshýd gloried and drank deep.* Ruins of an empire. Perhaps if the Shah had not held that infamous party, none of this would have happened. Millions spent, monarchs, presidents, sultans, ambassadors, movie stars, all invited to Persepolis, to witness the greatness of the Persians. Decadence: 159 chefs, bakers, and waiters, all flown in from Paris. Roasted peacock, caviar, crystal, Limoges china. Thousands of snakes, scorpions and lizards, cleared from the site; zoologists took the unknown species away, packed into special jars. Pine trees were planted in the desert. *Bekhab Cyrus, ma beedareem.* Sleep on, Cyrus, we are awake.

Nightingales. Visiting Shiraz in 1932, Rabinderath Tagore wanted to hear the legendary *Bulbul of Shiraz*, but his trip fell at the wrong time of year. Anxious to please the famous poet, Mirza Ibrahim commissioned a mechanical bird to be made, containing a recording of the nightingale in full song. When you turned a handle, it would sing. Nightingale – symbol for poetry, lyric voice. *That ancient voice was heard at once by emperor and clown.* A voice to console the homesick. To soothe the heart of Ruth, standing in the alien corn. That Shiraz nightingale spoke to the Bengali poet in a language that was universal, at a time when the internationalist movement was in full swing. Tagore's great admirer Yeats described a mechanical nightingale in 'Sailing to Byzantium', *Of hammered gold and gold enamelling / To keep a drowsy Emperor awake; / Or set upon a golden bough to sing / To lords and ladies of Byzantium / Of what is past, or passing, or to come.*

Underneath an apple tree in Highgate, John Keats, inspired by a nightingale's song. In a wood on the edge of Helpston, a village on the brink of the Lincolnshire fens, John Clare, who shared a publisher with Keats, transcribed the nightingale's song in words. 1889, just over a decade after Clare's death, the first birdsong was recorded mechanically. Ludwig Koch, a precocious 8-year-old, made a recording on his father's phonograph. He was to arrive in England an exile from Nazi Germany in 1936. His recordings were acquired by the BBC and established the first natural history sound archive. Birdsong and exile. When you turn the handle, a nightingale still sings. A summer song, from long ago. A song of all that's passing.

Tehran, back again. Stranger to the place. Plane trees
still lined the boulevards, water still ran down from the
mountains in *joob* along the roadsides. In the park, a man
was still selling balloons. You could still smell corn on the
cob roasting on charcoal. The Japanese garden was still there,
with its ornamental trees and rocks and raked gravel. But the
park was renamed, *Laleh.* And the dress code had changed:
you had to look as drab as possible, to avoid notice. No bright
clothes. No make-up. I didn't mind wearing the *roosaree*
(head-scarf). It was an adventure. I was in disguise.

Sitting in our old flat on Boulevard Keshavarz (formerly
Boulevard Elizabeth) refusing to accept tea or sweets
(*Quality Street)* from the tenants who had claimed it as their
own. A modern, stylish flat. Earthquake proof. We had run
away, they said. We were never coming back. *Don't eat the
sweets,* my mother warned us. *Don't accept their hospitality.
They are trying to take our flat.* Persephone.

Behind the metal gates of my great-aunt's house, you could
wear what you wanted. We swam in the little pond and
watched my grandmother shell broad beans, hollowing out
watermelon skins for us to sail like boats on the little pond.
The watermelons arrived in an open-top truck and were
rolled down into the cellar. Every day she would take one and
cut it for us and make juice from what was left. The garden
had two tall dusty persimmon trees, the round orange fruit
high out of reach. There was a pomegranate. The gardener
said he'd cut off my nose if I picked one.

Inside was dark; a cool terrazzo floor. Sometimes, at night,
we'd hear the scuttle of cockroaches – *soosk* – their sickly
sweet smell. Upstairs, a room was always closed off. Rolled
up carpets. Mothballs. Boxes full of books, left behind. I sat

there in the half-light, reading, not *Lolita*, but a novel by de Sade. Bodies around a tree. How detached it seemed. How distant. Outside was fear.

Inside the contemporary art museum, a giant newspaper boat. Knives suspended from the ceiling.

Saddam was bombing Tehran. Mum told us the noise was thunder in the mountains. Then the windows shattered. Adults gathered around the radio. My great aunt refused to go into the cellar. If a bomb hit the house, she wanted to die straight away, not get trapped underground. Every night, sirens, bombs, anti-aircraft guns. Every morning, warm bread for breakfast, mint, feta cheese, hot tea. Sometimes crisp, cool *kharboozeh*, a pale green melon from Masshad. Very good with bread and cheese.

> *Noon o paneer o kharboozeh,*
> *Bokhor bebeen che khoshmaze!*

My dad would teach us the rhyme:

> *Bread and cheese and kharboozeh,*
> *Eat and see how delicious!*

It didn't work in translation.

Bombers were targeting the airport. As our plane took off, you could feel the relief, smell it: the adults all lit up.

Heathrow airport always smells the same: rubber, tarmac. We soon reached home. SW13. Its air of quiet moderation. Semi-detached houses with magnolia trees. Pancake races round the duck pond. Every spring, cherry blossom. Leafy, suburban. We were the noisy foreigners.

Thirteen days after Persian New year, *No-rooz*, we'd carry plates of wheatgrass down to the river and throw it in, to take the bad luck away, hoping no-one would notice or ask what we were doing. Little green islands floating towards the sea –

      Wapping,

   Greenwich,

       Tilbury.

ACKNOWLEDGEMENTS

I am grateful to the editors of the following publications in which some of these poems first appeared: *The London Magazine, The Oxford Gazette, Magma, The Delinquent, PN Review, International Literary Quarterly*. My thanks are due to the editors of the following anthologies, in which several of these poems were first published: *Herrings: A Poetry in Aldeburgh Anthology, Mimic Octopus: an anthology of Poetic Imitation,* Carcanet's *New Poetries V*.

'Migrants' refers to events described in a film made by Sarah Wood and Helen Macdonald, *Murmurations X*.